There Is Hope, Just Pause and Listen

A Collection of Short, God-Inspired Poems

Bianca Roman

WESTBOW
PRESS®
A DIVISION OF THOMAS NELSON
& ZONDERVAN

WestBow Press books may be ordered through booksellers or by contacting:

WestBow Press
A Division of Thomas Nelson & Zondervan
1663 Liberty Drive
Bloomington, IN 47403
www.westbowpress.com
844-714-3454

ISBN: 978-1-6642-1991-5 (sc)
ISBN: 978-1-6642-1993-9 (hc)
ISBN: 978-1-6642-1992-2 (e)

Library of Congress Control Number: 2021901526

Print information available on the last page.

WestBow Press rev. date: 04/07/2021

Foreword

The inspiration in writing these poems came from a place of tragedy and suffering that is an inevitable reality that many face through the process of life. Many of these poems were written by my personal experience along with that of others who have personally gone through trials and tribulations. In life, we are bound to face an array of challenges that result in emotions that are both good and bad. Despite the challenges we face, there is hope for all of us that God has a great love for us all. There is hope; just pause and listen.

The reflection page after each poem is for your personal thoughts and life experiences that connect you to that particular poem.

Testimony

Through my story you can see how big, great, and amazing our God is. He took an ordinary person like me who didn't like to read, let alone write, Christian poetry and used me for His glory. One afternoon I was just being my regular, plain self, feeling pretty down and praying to God to take me home. I was thinking that sometimes this life and everything that happens in it are too much. All of a sudden, my head started to fill with rhymes, and I didn't know what was going on. I started to write them down, and the rhymes were continuously resonating in my mind. After writing down these rhymes, a turtledove appeared on my deck. This bird would come every morning and leave at night. I felt as though its presence was like the Holy Spirit guiding me on what to write. Whenever this dove was not present, I did not have any rhymes in my mind. I was just an instrument used for God's glory.

The first poem in this compilation, which was the first one given to me, will describe to you exactly how I felt when the Holy Spirit started to fill my head with rhymes. As they kept coming, I felt more hope and peace coming over me. I think that God uses ordinary people like me to spread the Word, especially people who don't necessarily have a high level of education or talent. We don't have to second-guess God's plan for us; we just need to let him guide us. We just have to believe that there is hope. Just pause and listen—just as the title of this book says. We should be open and listen because many times life takes us away from the quiet of our minds.

Thank you for allowing me to share this miracle in my life with you.

Awaiting

I wait in the daylight,
I wait in the darkness,
I wait with patience.
Some days I'm anxious
Just to go home,
To be in peace,
To rest my soul,
And to be free.
To see your face,
O God of mine,
To hear your voice,
To remain calm,
And in that moment, with relief,
To say, "I'm home; I'm home indeed."

Reflections

_____
_____
_____
_____
_____
_____
_____
_____
_____
_____
_____
_____
_____
_____
_____
_____
_____
_____
_____
_____
_____
_____
_____
_____
_____
_____
_____
_____
_____

The Quiet after Rain

It's cold outside and pouring rain.
And in my mind, it feels the same.
But as I pray and close my eyes,
I'm feeling good—to my surprise.
My mind gets quiet as I feel
God's warm touch and soothing voice
Deep in my soul; I rejoice.
The rain in my mind is gone, but
Outside it is still pouring down with love.

Reflections

The Ear That Listens

I open my eyes, and I look around.
Not even a noise, not even a sound.
But I can hear a voice so clear.
Who could it be? There's no one near.
I try to close my eyes and listen
To the strange voice that won't quit whispering,
"I'm here, I'm here. Oh, child of mine,
You're not alone. You never were.
Good days or bad, you don't have to worry.
My arms are open in full glory.
I listen to your breaking voice,
To all your sorrows, to all your joy.
I'm always near to hold you tight.
Don't be afraid; you're a child of mine."

Reflections

Hallelujah

Hallelujah in the highest.
Hallelujah here on earth.
Hallelujah in my soul.
Hallelujah around the world.
Rejoice, rejoice, brothers and sisters.
Lift up your arms and voices with gladness.
Let's make ourselves heard
In joy and sadness.
Don't be afraid, and don't be shy.
Let's shout; His name be glorified
And all united in one voice.
Let's sing, let's pray, and let's rejoice.

Reflections

The Special Wood

A piece of wood and a few nails,
You look at them and wonder, *What's special?*
But when you put them all together
And build the cross that your sins carried,
It's very special, my dear friend, and it's not quite ordinary.
The holy body lay upon it—
Without a sin, without a stain—
To save an ordinary soul, to take my sins so far away,
And never ever to remember my shameless
ways, my days of wonder.
I'm just in awe of His great love;
I'm just in awe and out of yonder.

Reflections

Get in the Water

Let's go to the water,
Full of joy and laughter.
Let's forget the crying;
Let's forget the dying.
The price was paid for you and me;
The price was paid entirely
When on the cross at Golgotha,
He gave His life just to save mine.
Don't hesitate, my sister or my brother.
Don't hesitate; get in the water.
You come out clean, a brand-new you,
Full of new hope for what awaits.
When ready, staying at the gates
To meet our Savior, sisters, brothers,
Make the right choice—get in the water!

Reflections

When I Met Jesus

When I met Jesus, I was scared,
And not at all was I prepared.
But His calm voice and soothing presence
Give you hope; they give you essence.
He waits for you, so come as you are.
Just bring your heart; pour it all out.
And by the hand He'll always guide you.
He knows you'll fall, make more mistakes, but
He's always there, and he awaits
To pick you right back up again
And not let go until the end.

Reflections

Put Your Faith in God

We all have joy.
We all have sorrow.
We all are thinking about tomorrow.
What will it be? What will I eat?
Where will I live or go to work?
My kids are hungry, sometimes sad,
What can I do to make them laugh?
And then in all your days of worry,
You reach your breaking point.
Just bow your head, drop to your knees,
Pray out to God, and give Him praise.
Let Him handle all your worry,
Your food, and your shelter; shine His glory.
And lift yourself up, back up again.
He's greater than your closest friend.

Reflections

Who Do You Think You Are?

Who do you think you are
To judge a restless soul,
A poor and challenged person?
You think you're so much more.
We're all the same in the eyes of God;
We're all the same to your surprise.
Just look deep inside yourself, my friend,
And leave the judging to the end.
Leave it to God's almighty power.
He loves us all, broke down or poor.
He doesn't see your wealth or color,
Your race, your richness, or your dollars.
That's all I have to say, my friend.
We are all one when it's the end.

Reflections

Prayer to God

I pray to God to save my soul.
I pray to God to make me better,
To make me understand what matters.
To forgive all that I'm not,
And to give me time to get it right.
But time is flying, so it's life.
Your time is now to do what's right.
He'll wrap you in His arms so tight.
Don't have to worry, just surrender,
And all your prayers will be answered.

Reflections

What Happens When
You Have God?

What's the worst that can happen?
What can they do to you?
They cannot touch your soul
When God is next to you.
They cannot drag you down
And roll you through the mud.
They're all hands of mortals
Your God would not allow.
He'll dry up all your tears
And heal up all your wounds.
He'll hold your hand forever,
Will never let it go.
When you are in His presence,
You'll never feel alone.

Reflections

The Greatest Date of Your Life

You think you have it all—
Good job, nice house, a car.
But I don't think you've had
The greatest date of all.
It's not going to a movie
Or to an ice-cream shop.
It's right here, close to you,
Right in your own backyard.
It is a date with Jesus
And all there is to gain.
It's free—just go on it—
And you might feel impressed.
He only wants your heart for everlasting life.
Just go on as you are,
No need for a suit and tie.
He'll walk you through, stay right beside you.
Just rest your head, and let Him guide you.

Reflections

Humility

Humility, what a great thing.
It's kind of rare in today's world.
Along with humbleness, kindness, and compassion.
It's hard to bow your head with passion.
But see the Light, and let it free you.
You'll learn those words again, you'll see.
And then start with yourself and live them
In your own life, and don't just preach them.
Be kind, be humble, and be a gem.
All you can be, a great I am.
Hold out your hand and help a stranger
And say a prayer; think of the manger
Where our dear Savior was born,
The most kind and humble soul.
We all should learn right from the Master
How to be humble, kind, compassionate.

Reflections

Don't Cry

Don't cry. He's ready when you are.
His patience, big; His love is greater.
He's always waiting there to greet you
With open arms and with no judgment,
With no big steps and no harassment.
He loves you just the way you are—
No need for a mask or a façade.
Just be yourself, and let Him hold you.
He'll wash you clean and will restore you.

Reflections

You

You think you're great,
A know-it-all.
Don't need salvation—you have people!
But when the time is getting near,
And you start feeling lots of fear,
Where are your people?
They desert you.
They let you down and leave you wondering.
They all start running, hiding.
There's only one who is still standing
Right by your side and patiently waiting
For you to just accept His love,
A better friend like no one else.

Reflections

Believe

How do you believe
When you doubt every step,
When you doubt every prayer,
When you are in despair?
You can call yourself a Christian,
But you don't trust Him fully.
Just let Him set you free.
Let Him to shine His glory.
Believe with all your heart,
No reason to have doubt,
And put your trust in Him.
He'll answer every prayer.
You just have to believe!

Reflections

Creator

Do you hear the quiet deep down in your head?
Do you feel your heart beating without stopping?
How do you think that happens?
You think it's just pure magic or just completely science?
Now let me tell you all,
All skeptics out there,
Nothing will ever move,
Not even a hair.
There is a greater power;
His name, almighty God
And the name of His Son, you know it, Jesus Christ.
He's bigger than the science,
More powerful than nature.
And let me tell you why.
It's all His great creation—
You and me, the birds, the sky,
Everything that's moving
Down here or way up high.

Reflections

Come to Jesus

Come to Jesus, all you out there,
Lonely, tired, in despair.
He'll hold you close, closer than ever.
He'll wipe your brow and make it better.
He'll make you fishermen of people.
A friend, a brother, or a sister
To someone in a greater need.
He'll give you words and what to speak.
Just rest your head in His warm hands.
At last you're found before the end.

Reflections

Angel

(Dedicated to Roxana)

A little girl, seven weeks old,
She's gone without a warning.
Her parents crying in despair
To God, "Why, God? It is not fair.
We were so happy, so in love.
Our little girl was perfect.
Why did You take her little soul?
Our little perfect angel.
I should be mad, so mad at You,
But strangely I am not.
Instead I pour my heart to You.
I'm quieting my mind
And letting Your peace and hope surround me.
I'll never let You go.
I'm sure Your plan for us is greater
Than our minds can hold.
I think You needed one more angel
In Your big and holy choir,
So I can hear the songs at night,
When I'm in peace and quiet."

Reflections

We're All One

Why is there so much pain?
Why is there so much sorrow?
Why can't we get it straight?
Why can't we see what matters?
The wars won't stop; the kids are dying.
Stop all the madness; stop all the crying.
Let's hold our hands together,
In prayer let's unite.
Let's ask our God Almighty
To make us get it right.
To help us love each other,
To be there, be a friend.
To open up our eyes and see we're all the same
Regardless of our color or of our social status
For in the eyes of God,
It's all a big hiatus.

Reflections

The Greater Power

You're waking up in a dark place,
Not knowing how you got there.
It pulls you down, it drags you under,
Makes you forget, and makes you wonder.
Is there escaping from it all?
Is there a greater power watching
And always ready just to catch me?
You hear His voice and take small steps,
Not sure what's there and what awaits.
But as you grow, the voice is clearer.
Just wants to help, make it all better.

Reflections

Be Humble

When you do something good for people,
Expect nothing in return.
Do it just because you want to.
Do it just because you could.
Don't go around telling out loud
To every ear that wants to listen
Of all the good that you've been doing,
Helping a brother or a sister.
Remember about the great example,
Which was Jesus on the cross.
He gave His life because He loved you.
You gave Him nothing, nor you could.

Reflections

Patience

You cannot live their lives
Or make them understand.
But just be there for them,
A mentor, a good friend.
And when their time is coming,
They'll turn their lives to God
For God, He loves us all,
No matter what we've done.
He'll turn your life around
And make you see the light.
You'll rise up from the ashes
Way better, with clear sight.
Then finally walk together,
Holding His mighty hand.
The path is narrow, there will be struggles,
But you will make it to the end.

Reflections

New Hope

Though my heart is broken
And my spirit crushed,
And I only see the bottom,
The dark and rumbling clouds,
I feel you in that darkness
And how you try to reach me.
If only I'll be clay
And let your love teach me.
If only I put aside
All of my dark and demons
And then listen to the whisper, the nice voice in my head,
The one that gives me hope,
Power, courage, and strength.
Forgetting all the past,
Start walking towards the light.
Now finally I can rest
My head in peace at night.

Reflections

Trust Him

Do you remember Daniel
Into the pit of lions?
And how he trusted God
And knew he wouldn't be dying?
He kept praising His name,
Trusting in Him, and obeying.
He knew that God was with him,
That he wouldn't be delaying.
He shut the mouth of lions
And make them like a kitten.
He'll do the same for you
Without a hesitation.
Just call His name out loud
In any situation.
He'll come to rescue you
And bring you your salvation.

Reflections

I Will See You Again

One day life hit me, hit me so hard
I didn't know what to do.
I lost the apple of my eye,
My rock, all that I knew.
Without him, I didn't see the light.
In my own pain and sorrow,
How am I supposed to live
Or think about tomorrow?
With every day, the healing came
To lift me up a bit
And make it through another day
To see the light, to see His way.
My heart still aching, but I have hope.
The days are passing by.
I cannot wait, my dearest Lord,
To wave this world goodbye.

Reflections

_____

_____

_____

_____

_____

_____

_____

_____

_____

_____

_____

_____

_____

_____

_____

_____

_____

_____

_____

_____

_____

_____

_____

_____

_____

_____

_____

_____

_____

_____

_____

_____

_____

_____

Just a Girl

Was just a girl holding the hands of her father and little brother.
She won't completely understand.
What was all the bother?
People around her crying,
And all wearing black
Her mother just there lying
In the deep and empty grave.
The little girl grew older,
Not even old enough
When tragedy struck her again,
Taking her only father,
The only one she knew,
And left her just with brother.
They were two kids alone—
No parents, very scared.
They had to grow up fast,
Be ready, be prepared
To grow and to be strong.
Much stronger than others
For life won't wait for them,
Not with a golden platter.
But if you see today,
How life for them is looking,
You would have to smile and say, "There's
God. He's not forgetting."

Reflections

_____

_____

_____

_____

_____

_____

_____

_____

_____

_____

_____

_____

_____

_____

_____

_____

_____

_____

_____

_____

_____

_____

_____

_____

_____

_____

_____

_____

_____

_____

_____

_____

If Only

If only I would be pretty,
If only I would be richer,
If only I would be taller,
My feet a little smaller.
There is so many ifs
Spinning in my head
That I keep forgetting
Just to live instead.
Look in the mirror, you.
You're beautiful, you're precious.
Why can't you understand
You're God's perfect creation,
His most important work.
Unique, a piece of art.
He loves you as you are.
Just give Him all your heart.

Reflections

Who's Knocking?

Answer the knock.
Don't be afraid.
Don't keep your heart in locking.
Don't want to miss the special knock.
Just open, stop withholding.
See who is there and what awaits.
Who's on the other side?
Let Him come in and make you whole.
Let Him touch your heart.
And hand in hand you will be walking
With Jesus by your side,
You'll have a Father and a friend
For the rest of your life.
Aren't you happy that you opened
The door that was in locking?
Aren't you glad, my dearest friend,
That you heard that knocking?

Reflections

_____
_____
_____
_____
_____
_____
_____
_____
_____
_____
_____
_____
_____
_____
_____
_____
_____
_____
_____
_____
_____
_____
_____
_____
_____
_____
_____
_____
_____

Dear Friend

(Dedicated to Ethel)

I love you, and you know it,
My good and dearest friend.
Even when we're not talking
Or see you weeks on end,
I know you're there for me
And hold me in your heart.
I do the same for you
Even when we're apart.
Your friendship is so priceless;
It means a lot to me.
I thank God every day
He put you in my way.
I know He blessed us both
With having one another.
He knows what we all need,
It's caring for each other.
A good friend, it's so rare,
It's like the rarest gem.
I pray for you, my dear,
I know you'll do the same.

Reflections

Rainbow after Rain

(Dedicated to Ofelia)

She was weeping in silence
When no one could hear it,
And begging of God,
"Please take this. I can't bear it.
I don't want my girls to grow up like this,
To think that this is normal
And not have bigger dreams.
I cry out to You, and I praise You every day.
Why can't You hear my prayers
And take it all away?"
"Patience, my child, I hear you.
I have a plan in place.
You just have to obey me,
And let me shine my grace.
I'll take you out of here,
Some place so good and new.
I'll hold you in My hand
And make you all brand-new."

Reflections

I Do

It is your happy day,
The day you say, "I do."
Make sure that you will sow
The love of God
Between the two.
And the three of you together,
Embarking on the life,
Some days the road is narrow,
And some days it is wide.
No matter what life brings you,
Hold tight onto each other.
Don't let the darkness stir you
Away from one another.
Don't let it steal your peace
And get between you.
Just step back and remember
The day you said, "I do."

Reflections

_____

_____

_____

_____

_____

_____

_____

_____

_____

_____

_____

_____

_____

_____

_____

_____

_____

_____

_____

_____

_____

_____

_____

_____

_____

_____

How Dare We?

How do we dare to judge
Just looking at the outside?
We do not know the struggle
And all that is inside.
The road of open hearts,
It takes so many paths.
Sometimes it's full of great things,
Sometimes full of regrets.
Remember just one story,
The one with that poor woman—
The one who everybody
Was so ready to stone?
They all picked up the rocks
To throw at her, to kill her
Because she was different,
In shame and just a loner.
So if you think you're perfect,
Go on, spit out your judging,
And you will find yourself
Alone and with your grudging.

Reflections

Thank You

How do I put this into words?
My gratitude for you, so big.
My arms are stretched out to the sky,
With all I have: Be glorified!
You changed my life
And made me whole.
Opened my eyes not to ignore
The little things that really matter.
You changed my heart.
You made me better.
I want to be like You,
To love and to forgive like You,
To be a wholesome person
Forever close to You.
And from the bottom of my heart,
I owe you a big, "Thank You."

Reflections

Be Yourself

I can't change my beliefs
So I can please the world.
Or put on a façade
'Cause not of it it's worth.
I can't lose my salvation
And all that is to come.
You are my restoration,
The only one I want.
Your gift for me, it's priceless.
It's something you can't buy.
There's no one else above You.
You gave Your life just to save mine.

Reflections

_____

_____

_____

_____

_____

_____

_____

_____

_____

_____

_____

_____

_____

_____

_____

_____

_____

_____

_____

_____

_____

_____

_____

_____

_____

_____

_____

_____

_____

I'm Here

Let Me heal your heart,
No matter how deep the cut.
Let Me come in and mend it all.
It's all taken apart;
I'll put it back together,
Help you heal all your wounds.
I'll stay with you forever,
No matter what happens.
I'll be there in your darkest days,
When tears fall from your eyes.
I hear your voice and feel your pain,
Don't doubt I'm there in every way.
I'll be there when you're full of joy
And laughter fills your heart.
The two of us together
Can manage every part.

Reflections

His Great Love

I want to live my life
The way You want me to.
I want to make You proud
To do all I can do.
To be a ray of hope
In this unfaithful world.
To be a grain of salt
To show others God's love
And teach them Your name's worth.
Why do we have to suffer
And keep wiping our tears
When You already paid the price
And set all of us free?
Just open up our eyes
So we can see the truth,
To let Your love to flood us,
Be happy and anew.

Reflections

He's Always Next to You

God is on your side.
There is no need to fear.
You're so valuable to Him,
He loves you and forgives.
He sees your deepest fears,
And He knows your heart.
You're most precious to Him.
Don't let this fall apart.
His love for you, it is so great.
It's selfless and unique.
He knows that you will make mistakes,
But He will not critique.
Instead He's always there for you
With open arms, ready to listen.
Lay down your head on His wide shoulder,
And let Him take your burden.

Reflections

_____

_____

_____

_____

_____

_____

_____

_____

_____

_____

_____

_____

_____

_____

_____

_____

_____

_____

_____

_____

_____

_____

_____

_____

_____

_____

_____

_____

_____

_____

_____

You Be the Difference

Don't think that you're too small
To do something, to make a difference.
Or you're not rich enough.
Just take small steps, be patient.
We all can be the change
To make a better world.
Just please look left and right;
There's something to be done.
If you just say a prayer
For somebody in need,
It helps them so much more.
It brings you to your knees.
Just hold a hand or lend a shoulder.
Be there and hear the crying.
Together with the love of God,
Let's change this, let's keep trying.

Reflections

Keep on Fighting

The world is your battlefield.
You, a very strong soldier,
Together with God's army
Can conquer every corner
Armed with love and with kind words.
You're pushing forward, not backward,
Touching hearts along the way
And changing lives.
You fight His way,
Not with a gun
And not with violence.
Just with a prayer and in silence.
You know that you can change the world
With love, kindness, and His Word.
Don't you give up.
Keep up your fighting.
You will prevail.
It's all in writing.

Reflections

Why?

We always see the why—
Why me? Why this? Why now?
We do not understand
What God for us has planned.
He's holding all the answers
To our desperate whys.
If only we had patience
And let Him be the guide.
It's all mapped out for you
Ever since you were born,
The path your life is taking.
He's the One in control.
When you fall down,
He'll pick you up.
He's there, and He is waiting.
Just come to Him,
You little child.
He knows what is awaiting.

Reflections

God's Remedy for Fear

What God gave me
You cannot take.
I'm sure He did not make mistakes.
He knows my heart,
He knows my dreams,
And everything that's right for me.
I let Him guide me,
Show me the path,
The only one that I should take.
No matter how many times I fall,
No matter how many walls I hit,
He'll pick me up from there.
His love for me ... so rare.

Reflections

Love Is the Answer

Love one another says
The greatest command of all.
But what do we all do?
Ignore it; we all stall.
Wake up, you tired souls
Asleep deep down inside.
Let's put aside our differences.
Wake up and see what's right.
Open your eyes and hearts.
Make room for love, not hate.
Because for all I know,
To hate is not okay.
Instead of seeing faults in someone else
And always be so ready to hate and criticize,
Please just show love and show compassion
Because I know love's the right answer.

Reflections

Let's All Be One

Let's hold our hands together—
Black, yellow, and white.
No barriers of religion
Can stop the love inside.
The love can conquer all,
Can break down all the barriers.
The outside is too small;
The inside is what matters.
So stop judging and saying,
"They are so different than me,"
Because God created us all.
Look through His eyes and see.
He sees us all the same,
Inside just one heart beating.
I dare you, and I pray.
"Look through His eyes," I say.

Reflections

Please, God

Please, please, please, please, dear Lord,
I'm praying and imploring.
I want to change the world,
Make it more peaceful, not ignoring.
I want to stop the wars, the violence, and the hate.
I want to see kids fed, with big smiles on their faces.
And girls going to school and having bigger dreams.
Make it safer to walk to pray and just to sing.
To wipe the dark aside, make room for the sun,
And all of us together to laugh and to have fun.
To praise Your name and dance
With our hands stretched high.
Please, God, answer my prayer.
Your power can't be denied.

Reflections

_____
_____
_____
_____
_____
_____
_____
_____
_____
_____
_____
_____
_____
_____
_____
_____
_____
_____
_____
_____
_____
_____
_____
_____
_____

I Love You, Lord

I spin around
And jump for joy
In the big field that's wet from dew.
In awe at how big Your love is,
Amazed that I belong to You.
Another day that You allowed me
Just to enjoy Your big creation.
Another day my eyes are open
And filled with love and admiration
For You're so good, so good to me.
Your hand, it's always stretched
So I can reach it when I'm down.
To grab it and confess
How great You are, how much You love me.
You're always by my side
When I am sad or in great pain.
You're never far behind.

Reflections

My Child

Be still, my child.
I hold your hand,
No need for you to worry.
I feel your heartbeat,
Hear your thoughts.
Your mind is full of worry.
Just lay your head down in my palms.
Quiet your busy mind.
You'll see the shadows lifting,
You'll feel the bright, warm sun.
Just drop your heavy load
Down at my feet; I'll say,
"I'll carry it for you.
I have already paid
For all of this and so much more
So you can have your freedom
To sing to pray and to be loved,
And just to know you are enough."

Reflections

This Is Who I Am

This is who I am,
As flawed as I may be.
It's not for you to judge it
Or pretend you don't see.
God, love me for me
And not some made-up story.
He made me all unique
So He can shine His glory
To use me for His good
In many different ways.
It may be through a poem
Or through a song, I say.
He gave us all a purpose,
A gift; we have to use it
To pray for others, lend a hand,
To spread His love and choose it.

Reflections

A Little Voice Inside Your Mind

A little voice inside your mind
Won't let you feel you're free.
You feel so different, you're so shy,
You think your place is not here.
But don't you worry, little soul,
You're so precious to me.
Don't listen to that old, mean voice
'Cause you belong to me.
I love you just the way you are,
With all your flaws and imperfections.
You look so perfect, so demure.
You are my own reflection.

Reflections

Your Legacy Behind

Why are we running on this earth
To climb the social ladder
When all this race for earthly things will not even matter?
It's all in vain, a fake assurance.
We think it makes us better.
But when we're gone, gone from the earth,
They all forget the ladder.
The only thing they will remember
Won't be your social status.
Will be the good you left behind in all this hiatus.
So please be good and humble.
Show love to all the people.
Your legacy behind you
Will be as strong as the tall steeple.

Reflections

You Are Worth It

I feel so small and so alone,
So lost in this big world.
I'm always drawn to the wrong places
To try to find my worth.
I think nobody misses me
When I am gone awhile.
Nobody says, "I love you,"
Or cares if I'm alive.
Until one day I heard a voice
I've never heard before
And thought, *What do you want from me?*
I have nothing, I'm not worthy.
But then the voice got clearer,
And all of it made sense.
It was my spirit talking,
"Come on, get up, now is your chance.
Start walking towards the light.
Forget your past, your demons.
You are so worth it, so unique.
You can start fresh, better believe."

Reflections

Second Chances

You have a second chance
To rise up from the ashes.
Your dreams cannot be over.
Don't you give up; you're precious.
You are a fighter, you are strong,
You are so many things.
And you are not a quitter.
That's not the way you think.
Don't let them drag you down
And tell you otherwise.
Don't listen to the voices
That spin inside your mind.
You know yourself, and so does God.
He made you to be strong.
He gave you a purpose.
You know He's never wrong.

Reflections

With God by My Side

I turn and toss and cannot sleep.
I try to find my peace.
But with so many worries,
I cannot feel at ease.
Alone I'll always have
A big weight on my shoulder.
It's time for me to let it go.
Be free, just drop that boulder.
But how, I do not know.
Alone I cannot do it.
I need God's power by my side.
Together we can do it.
His love will lift me up.
His kindness will surround me.
That boulder on my shoulder,
It's crumbling down behind me.

Reflections

No Permission Needed

I do not need permission so I can love God.
Nor do I need a title; I know that I'm His child.
He's there for me and listens to everything I say.
His kindness and His love
They're here for me to stay.
He is my help, my rock.
Whenever I am down—
No matter if it's morning
Or very late at night—
The One that I can call without hesitation
When I am happy or I'm sad,
In any situation.

Reflections

I Lift My Eyes to the Blue Sky

And wonder if You're there.
Is that the heaven where You're living?
Oh wait ... it can't be there.
You're all around me, everywhere,
All over the world.
The universe, it's Yours,
And everything it holds.
The universe, it's Yours—
The beauty that surrounds me,
The breeze, and the warm fun,
The rainbow up above,
The ocean's wave, the clouds.
They're all made by Your hands
And the sound of Your voice.
They all just listen, not ignore.

Reflections

God, What a Perfect Day

God, what a perfect day
To wake up in the morning,
To see that the sun is rising,
And birds are singing to Your glory.
I'm blessed, and I'm in awe
To see all that surrounds me.
You granted me another day.
"Thank You, my Father," I shall say.
I'll join the birds in singing,
Together praise Your name.
I'm glad that I'm alive
To pray and love and live Your way.
All that You do is perfect.
It's beautiful and splendid.
It doesn't need retouching.
I let myself emerge in it.

Reflections

You Go in Hiding for a While

You go to hiding for a while
And try to hide your face.
You think that if nobody sees you,
They will forget the shame.
You are in pain, and you are hurting
For everything you've done.
People around still talking;
It doesn't look like they'll every stop.
Your friends, they weren't friends.
They left you when you needed them.
You're on your own to figure out
How to do better and keep living,
To pick up all the pieces
That are left from your life
And mend them back together.
You think nobody's by your side,
But there's the love of God.
He is your real, dear friend.
No matter what you've done,
He'll always hold your hand.
He'll stay with you forever,
Help you pick up the pieces
And put them back together.

Reflections

Just Say Thank You Every Day

Just say thank you every day
For whatever comes your way.
See the light in all the things,
No matter how hard it seems.
They're all just lessons,
And they teach us
How to be patient and to trust.
To give our worries to the Father
And see the rainbow in every cloud.
There is a rainbow in every cloud.

Reflections

Thank You, Lord, for This Birthday

Thank You, Lord, for this birthday.
I thank You, my dear Lord,
For listening to my prayers
And knowing all that I need.
I thank You for the gift
You sent me one October.
She's like a blessing in my life.
And I'll always remember
Her heart is always kind,
Her spirit is always kind.
And when I need a ear to listen,
She's there without complaining.
Yeah, it is true she likes to travel
And to see the wonders of Your hands.
But everywhere she goes
She praises Your name with her friends.
Today it is her day, a very special one.
The day You mapped her future,
The day her life began.
Another year is going by.
She's wiser with the time.
I thank You once again for her.
The privilege, it's mine.

Reflections

How I Need You

How I need You.
I need Your love like I need water.
I need forgiveness like I need sun.
Just keep me in Your arms,
Oh, God of mine, oh, God of mine.
Please never let me go
'Cause without You, I am a stranger.
I have no purpose in this world.
I feel so lost and feel endangered.
You are the One who keeps me safe
And always walks with me
In sunny days or rain.
No matter what life brings,
You blessed me from the beginning
And gave me all I need,
A purpose in my life.
With joy for You I sing.
Your love is so amazing.
Your arms are always stretched
To catch me when I fall
And lift me back right on my path.

Reflections

Trust Me

Trust me,
One day you're stuck in life,
So lonely and confused.
You feel like an orphan
With nothing left to lose.
Your life is crumbling down
Right before your eyes.
You yell in desperation to God,
"Where are You now?
I need You, God. I need You.
I'm ready to give up.
I do not have the power
Or the desire to look up.
But then I feel Your hand
And hear Your soothing voice."
"It's not the end of the road for you.
That's something I control.
Just stay with Me forever,
And let your heart to trust Me.
With Me by your side,
I will forever guide you."

Reflections

I Don't Know
What Tomorrow Brings

I don't know what tomorrow brings
Or if it will be better.
All that I know is there is grâce.
And we have to finish this race
Here on this earth to make it home,
To make it a better place.
Don't gather treasure here, my friend.
It would be useless; you won't need it.
Just focus on your destination,
Where all is peaceful and no damnation.
Come as you are; don't try to hide
Your flaws or imperfections.
He'll wash you clean, a brand-new you.
He is your restoration.

Reflections

Show Me Your Ways

Lord, show me Your ways,
And I'll try to follow.
I may not be perfect.
Some days I'm down and shallow.
But You never give up
And point me right again.
You hold me by the hand
And teach me how to stand.
When I am mad at You,
You never turn Your back.
Just show me love and patience
And teach me what You can.
You make me understand
That all is with purpose.
And that wondering on earth,
It's temporary and it's mirthless.
When I get home at last
And stand in front of You,
I'll finally exhale and tell You how much I love You.

Reflections

You Knew Me before I Was Born

You knew me before I was born.
You knew I'd mistakes.
You put Your fingerprint on me
And showed me what it takes.
Without You I'd be like a lead
That rides the wave of the wind,
Carried into the unknown,
Not knowing where to land.
I'm happy that You found me
And hold me by Your side.
With You I feel secure.
I'm not afraid when You decide.
Whatever comes my way,
You're always near and hold me.
In prayer I rejoice.
I know You're close; You told me.

Reflections

I Wanna Gaze at Your Beauty

I wanna gaze at Your beauty,
At the beauty of Your temple.
The beauty of the cross
Where blood was shed for my salvation.
Without Your sacrifice,
I would still be a mortal.
I would not feel the love
Or know what's important.
I'd be so lonely and confused,
No purpose or direction.
I'd be a troubadour in life
Full of wonder and rejection.
But thanks to You, my Lord,
And Your big sacrifice,
My eyes are now wide open.
I see the light; it's not surprise.

Reflections

It's Cold Outside and Very Quiet

It's cold outside and very quiet.
The snowflakes dance in the sky.
I see the flicker of a light
In a small house just on the side.
I hear the noises from inside,
A joyful laugh and giggles.
And as I peek through the small window,
I see a Christmas tree and glitter.
I pause just for a moment
And wonder with surprise
If all those people there inside,
If they do know the love of Christ.
I wonder if the Christmas for them is just a tree
Full of glitter and big presents,
Another holiday they see.
I'm hopin' and I'm praying they understand the day.
It's one of big importance,
When our Lord was born to save.

Reflections

The Road Was Long and Hard

The road was long and hard,
And Mary was almost ready
To give birth to our Lord.
They had to go, keep steady.
When finally they arrived
In small town Bethlehem,
Nobody wanted to help them.
They were so lonely and so scared.
But then they found a place,
Just a tiny manger
With cows to keep them warm
And out of sight of danger.
Then in that humble place,
Our dear Savior was born
To bring us peace and joy,
To walk with us on earth.

Reflections

Printed in the United States
by Baker & Taylor Publisher Services